A TREASURY OF ASIAN FOLKTALES

Retold by **Linda Gan**
Illustrated by **Kwan Shan Mei**

EARLYBIRD BOOKS
An imprint of Federal Publications (S) Pte Ltd
A member of the Times Publishing Group
Times Centre, 1 New Industrial Road, Singapore 1953

© **1991 Federal Publications (S) Pte Ltd**

ISBN 981 01 0154 6

Printed in Singapore

earlybird books

The Author

LINDA GAN teaches in the Department of Specialised Education at the Institute of Education, Singapore. She taught in London for more than ten years before coming to live in Singapore in 1979. Mrs Gan has written a number of books and readers for the Curriculum Development Institute of Singapore and is the author of the *Times Vocabulary Builders* series published between 1988 and 1990. She is married and has a baby boy.

The Illustrator

KWAN SHAN MEI is Singapore's most highly acclaimed illustrator of children's books. Born in China and educated in Shanghai, this gifted artist has done extensive research on Oriental costumes. She has received many awards and commendations for her work in children's books, among them the Gold Medal at the 1980 Singapore Festival of Books, the 1980 Noma Concours for Children's Picture Book Illustrations (administered by the Asian Cultural Centre for UNESCO), and an Honourable Mention in the Biennale of Illustrations Bratislava (BIB) in 1973. Her illustrations have a lyrical beauty and she is highly talented in delineating both emotions and scenery.

CONTENTS

THE EMPEROR AND THE NIGHTINGALE

L ong ago, in the garden of the Emperor Wu's splendid palace in China, there lived a nightingale. It sang so sweetly that all who heard it agreed that what they liked most in this garden was the nightingale's singing.

One day, the Emperor of Japan came to visit
Emperor Wu and he, too, fell in love with the
nightingale's songs. When he returned home he
wrote a letter to Emperor Wu saying that his
favourite memory of his visit to China had been
the nightingale's singing.

5

Emperor Wu was very surprised to hear this because he had never heard the nightingale sing before! He immediately ordered his servants to bring this wonderful bird to him. He enjoyed its singing so much that he insisted on keeping it near him in his palace.

Many months passed and the nightingale kept Emperor Wu very happy until one day, the Emperor of Japan sent him a little toy bird which could sing and dance. Emperor Wu became so fascinated by this bird that he completely forgot about the nightingale.

The poor nightingale felt so sad and unwanted that it flew away from the palace and for a whole year no one saw it and no one heard its lovely singing.

Then one day, the toy bird suddenly stopped singing and dancing. Toymakers from all over the land came to the palace to try and mend it but the toy bird lay still and silent.

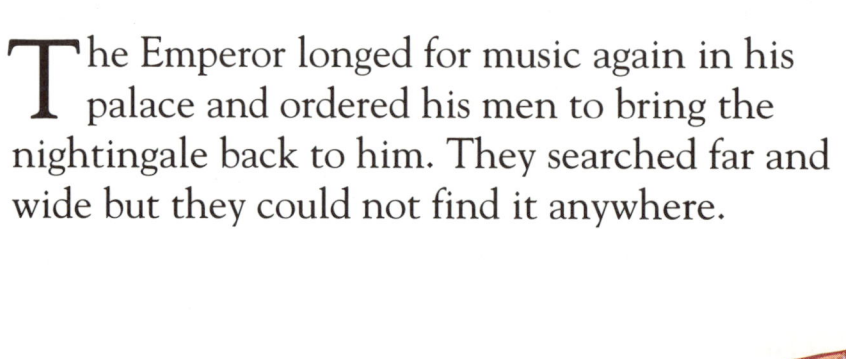

The Emperor longed for music again in his palace and ordered his men to bring the nightingale back to him. They searched far and wide but they could not find it anywhere.

The Emperor became sadder and sadder with each day that passed. He stopped eating and sleeping and just lay in his bed waiting to die.

Then one night, the Emperor heard a bird
singing so sweetly outside his bedroom that he
was sure it was the nightingale. He slowly sat up in
bed and tears started to roll down his cheeks, for
there on the window sill sat his beloved
nightingale.

"Stay with me dear nightingale," he whispered,
"and I promise I will never neglect you again."

From that day on, the nightingale stayed in the
palace and its sweet singing made the Emperor well
again and kept him happy and contented for the
rest of his life.

THE UGLY BOATMAN

O nce upon a time, there lived a young boatman by the name of Truong Chi. He was a very kind man but extremely ugly. He led a lonely life and spent his time fishing and playing the flute. All who heard his music fell in love with it.

The beautiful daughter of a Mandarin Lord
adored his music. Every evening, she waited for
his boat to pass by her window. When she heard the
sweet notes of his flute, her face sparkled with
happiness!

Her father was very unhappy about his daughter's
love for this poor boatman's music. He ordered
his men to lock all the windows in his mansion.
Truong Chi's music could no longer be heard and
the lovely girl grew sadder and sadder.

She became very ill and no doctor could help her. Her father feared she might die. He promised to give her anything she wanted. "Just the boatman's sweet music," she whispered.

The Mandarin Lord quickly summoned Truong
Chi to her bedside. The boatman's kind heart
ached when he saw the young girl so close to death.
He softly played his flute. A smile flickered across
her face and her parents knew she was better.

Then she opened her eyes and looked into
Truong Chi's face. She started to cry. Tears of
disappointment streamed down her cheeks.
"Oh!" she thought, "how could such an ugly man
play such beautiful music." Her parents begged
Truong Chi to help her. He knew why she was
crying and that he could do nothing more.

Truong Chi returned to his boat and his lonely life. He longed to see the Mandarin's daughter again but he knew this was impossible. He lost interest in everything, even his flute. Then one cold night, he fell ill. He grew weaker every day and he knew he was dying. Before he died, he asked that his heart be made into a cup for the Mandarin's daughter.

After Truong Chi died, all that remained of him was his heart of gold. It was made into a delicate golden cup and given to the Mandarin's daughter. She thought it was the loveliest thing she had ever seen.

She immediately filled the cup with tea and lifted it to her lips. Her heart suddenly froze! There in the cup she saw Truong Chi's shadow and heard his flute! The music was sweet at first, but then it changed. It sounded like the cry of a man with a broken heart. She let the cup slip from her grasp. It shattered into a thousand pieces and the music abruptly stopped.

Truong Chi's heart and his music were free forever. But not so the Mandarin's daughter. She never married. For the rest of her life she remained haunted by the boatman's tender love for her and his beautiful gentle music.

THE SUN KING

Once upon a time when the Earth was new, the sky hung so low that children could leap from the treetops and tumble and toss in the woolly clouds. The King of Siam ruled the Earth then, and his friend, the Sun King, ruled the heavens.

Every day, the Sun King's golden chariot would burn a blazing trail across the sky bringing light and warmth to the Earth.

When the Sun King returned to his palace amongst the clouds, night would fall. Then the tiny stars would come out to prick the soft darkness with their playful light, for at that time, there was no moon to brighten the night sky.

All was calm and peaceful on Earth and every one was very happy, especially the King and Queen of Siam for they had a beautiful child called Tatsani which means the Daughter of Dawn. As the years passed, Tatsani grew into a beautiful young woman.

One day, as she was playing in the palace gardens, the Sun King rode past in his chariot. He was so struck by her beauty that he could not bear to leave her side. From that moment, he remained on Earth driving his chariot round and round the palace to keep her beloved face in sight.

But this caused havoc on Earth! The constant sunlight made plants and fruit grow twice as fast and stopped the people from working and sleeping properly. "Oh," they cried, "why doesn't the Sun King return to his palace and bring us relief from this scorching heat and white bright sunlight?"

The stars were also thinking the same thing for without the dark of the night they could not come out to play. They decided to try to do something about it. An opportunity soon came. Tatsani went out for a walk one day and, finding a cave, she went inside to explore. The Sun King followed, leaving his chariot outside. There within the cave he confessed his great love for her.

The stars, meanwhile, shot down from the heavens and hid the King's chariot in thick bushes nearby. Cool darkness immediately wrapped itself around the Earth and the stars bounced happily in the night sky once again. The King realised something was very wrong and rushed out of the cave. There, to his great dismay, he found that his chariot had disappeared.

His great joy suddenly turned to great sorrow. He couldn't return home without his chariot, nor stay on Earth because he did not belong there. He knelt down and wept. Tatsani was so overcome with pity for him that she wept too. As their teardrops touched the ground the King's tears turned to gold and Tatsani's to silver. They have remained in the earth ever since as a precious reminder of these two lovers.

The stars watched all this in great distress as they, too, loved Tatsani and could not bear to see her cry. "Master of the Sun," they cried, in voices that tinkled in the velvet blackness. "Make us two promises and we will return your golden chariot."

The Sun King was relieved to find out who had stolen his chariot. "Ah, you little rascals," he said. "Go ahead and tell me what you want!"

"Firstly, you must promise to return home at the end of each day," the stars sang. "Secondly, give us Tatsani for half of every month to be the Moon, the Queen of the night."

The Sun King and Tatsani agreed. From that time on, he has always returned to his palace after circling the Earth every day. Tatsani then appears to keep her twinkly friends company. And when she is absent from the night sky you now know where she is, don't you?—cuddling her fiery husband in his palace in the clouds!

THE MAGICAL PRINCESS

Long ago in Malaysia, there lived a beautiful princess who could change herself into thirty different persons. Many men wanted to marry her but she refused all of them. Sultan Mahmud Shah of Malacca was one of these men. He sent his best friend, Hang Nadim, to ask her to be his wife.

Hang Nadim set forth with many precious gifts to find this magical princess. Her palace was on the top of Mount Ophir. It was covered with thick jungle and Hang Nadim and his servants found the journey very difficult.

Just as they were about to give up, an old woman dressed in black appeared. She was the Princess in disguise. "I have been sent to help you," she said. Suddenly a path of shining light cut through the jungle showing them the way to the top.

There they found the fair Princess sitting on a splendid throne of gold and silver. Hang Nadim told her of the Sultan's wish to marry her and gave her the gifts. The Princess was not impressed by them. "Tell your Sultan," she said, "that these gifts do not prove his love for me. Ask him to build a bridge of solid gold between our two kingdoms. Then I can visit my people whenever I want."

Hang Nadim returned to the Sultan with her demand. After much thought, he agreed to it because he wanted to marry her so much. The next day, he ordered his soldiers to collect gold from every person in the country.

Thousands of men toiled for seven days and seven nights to build the bridge. When Hang Nadim took the Princess to see it, she gasped in amazement. It glowed so brilliantly in the sun's golden rays. But she was still not satisfied. "Ask your Sultan to give me a cup of blood from his son's right hand," she said, "to show he truly loves me."

The Sultan was sadly silent when he heard this. Much to Hang Nadim's horror, though, he agreed. That same night both men crept into the boy's bedroom. Twice the Sultan raised his jagged kris to slash his son's wrist but each time he faltered.

He raised his deadly weapon again. Suddenly a flash of lightning ripped across the room and there stood the Princess. "I could never marry you," she said coldly to the Sultan, "because you were willing to kill your son in order to marry me."

Then, changing herself into thirty different persons, each one more beautiful than the last, she disappeared in another flash of lightning.

And so ends the tale of the magical Princess. She was never seen again and no trace was left of the Sultan's love for her. The beautiful golden bridge was swallowed up by the unfriendly jungle covering Mount Ophir. Some people believe the Princess still lives there, alone and unmarried. But unless someone climbs the mountain to check, we will never know, will we?

TARO & HIS GRANDMOTHER

Once upon a time in Japan, there lived a young farmer called Taro. He lived with his grandmother whom he loved very much. They and the other families in the village grew their own rice, wheat and vegetables. Usually there was plenty of food to feed everyone.

At the time of our story, however, no rain had fallen for many months and the wells had dried up and the crops had died. The villagers had very little food to eat.

The headman of the village, who had no family and lived alone, realised that there was not enough food for everyone. He decided that the young were the most important people in the village because they were strong and could work hard. He therefore ordered all the old people who were over the age of sixty to leave the village and go and live in the mountains.

Each family said a sad farewell to their old
relatives—all except Taro. He loved his
grandmother so much that he could not bear to
send her away. Unknown to anyone, he hid her in
a small room in his hut and secretly brought her
food to eat.

A few weeks later, the headman put up an important notice for everyone to read. It came from the warlord of another village who threatened to take away half the land in Taro's village unless the answers to three riddles could be found. If they could be solved, then he promised to give the villagers all the food they needed.

Taro quickly ran home to tell his grandmother the riddles. If she could solve them, then perhaps the headman would let her stay in the village.

"Grandmother," he said, "listen carefully to this first riddle: how can you tell which part of a log is nearer the top and which part is nearer the roots?"

The old woman thought for a while and then said: "Throw the log into the water. The part nearer the roots will sink and the part nearer the top will float."

Taro was very happy with her answer and asked her the second riddle: "How can you make a rope of ashes?"

Again she thought for a while and then replied: "Take a strong rope and pour salt over it. Light it at one end and it will burn slowly until all that is left is a coil of ashes."

Taro was very excited. She had only one more riddle to solve! "Here is the last riddle," he said. "How do you run a silk thread through a hollow pipe which is curved and crooked?"

The old lady laughed. "Oh, that's simple!" she said. "Just tie one end of the thread round an ant's leg. Put some honey at one end of the hollow pipe and push the ant in the other end. The ant will try to get to the honey and as it does so, will pull the thread through the pipe, however curved and crooked it is!"

Taro jumped for joy! How lucky he was to have such a wise grandmother. He quickly rushed to the headman's house and told him the answers to the three riddles. The headman was amazed at how clever Taro was.

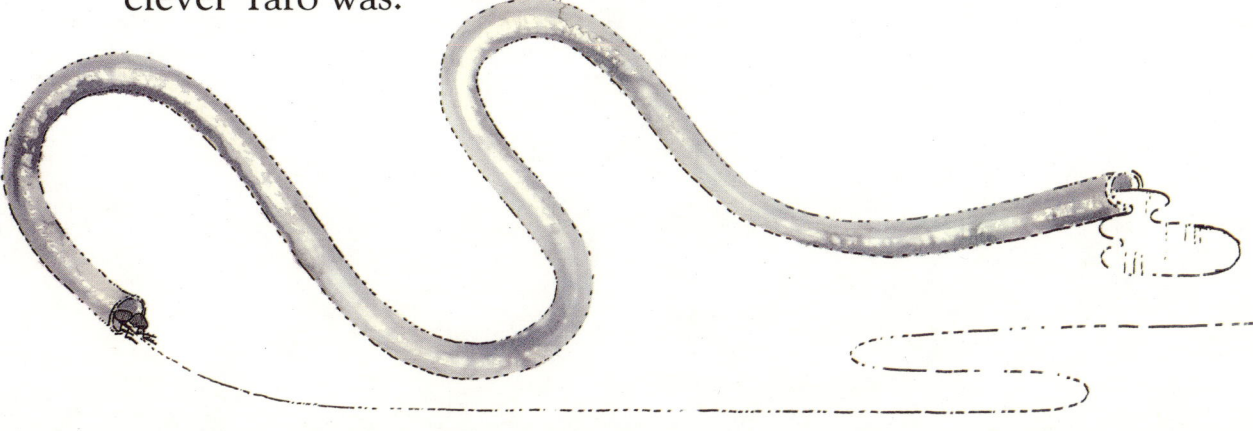

"Oh no, sir," Taro humbly said, "I did not solve the riddles. It was my dear old grandmother who gave me the answers."

The headman bowed his head in shame. He had always thought old people were stupid and useless. He thanked Taro and showered him with gifts for his grandmother.

Then he ordered his men to find all the old people he had turned out of the village and bring them back to live there again for as long as they wished. The old folk returned to their families and there was much rejoicing in the village.

Rain soon fell again and the wells filled up with water and the crops grew. From that day on the villagers lived a happy and prosperous life, thanks to Taro's wise old grandmother.

THE WHITE ELEPHANT

Many years ago in a small village in Myanmar, there lived a potter and a washerman. U Tin, the potter, was rather stupid and lazy. U Nam, the washerman, was just the opposite. He was hardworking and successful. U Tin was very jealous of the clever washerman.

One day, the King of Myanmar announced that he wished to own a white elephant. He already had many grey elephants, but he wanted a white one. This was because the people of Myanmar believed such animals were holy and only kings could own them.

U Tin seized this chance to make trouble for
U Nam. He told the King that U Nam could
wash a grey elephant until it turned white. The King
was very happy to hear this. He summoned the
washerman to his palace and ordered him to start
scrubbing his grey elephant immediately.

U Nam was very smart. He knew U Tin was behind all this and he quickly replied: "Your Majesty, I need a very big pot to wash your elephant in. I'm sure U Tin the potter can make it."

The King summoned U Tin to the palace. U Tin was horrified when he heard he had to make a pot large enough to hold an elephant! He and his family quickly set to work. The first pot they made broke because the elephant was too heavy for it! So they made a thicker pot.

Much to everyone's surprise it didn't break. But U Nam refused to start washing the animal until the water was boiling hot. So the King's men built an enormous fire under the pot. Many hours passed but the water was still cold. The King became impatient and demanded to know why the water would not boil. U Nam calmly explained that the pot was too thick.

The King therefore ordered U Tin to make another pot. Poor U Tin worked frantically for many months. He made many pots of all sizes and thicknesses but not one was suitable. The King was very angry with the potter for making him look such a fool. He decided he didn't want a white elephant any more and ordered U Tin to leave the country.

The potter sadly left Myanmar and went in search of work elsewhere. His silly jealousy had ruined his life. U Nam's quick wit on the other hand had helped him to lead a happy and peaceful life for the rest of his days.

THE BIRD HUNTER

Once upon a time in Indonesia, there lived a poor bird hunter. His name was Wajan. He dreamed of marrying Bintang Devi, the most beautiful girl in the land. She was the daughter of Raja Ishak, the King of Indonesia.

Raja Ishak was a keen archer. He loved the sport so much that he wanted his daughter to marry the best archer in the country. Wajan, unfortunately, knew nothing about archery. But he was clever and worked out a plan to marry her.

He caught some wild birds and plucked out their right eyes. Then he took them to the palace gates and tried to sell them. A crowd gathered around him. The King sent a servant to find out what was going on.

When he heard about the one-eyed birds, he summoned Wajan to him. "How is it," he asked Wajan, "that all your birds have only one eye?"

Wajan cleverly replied, "Your Majesty, I always shoot my birds in the right eye."

The King was amazed at Wajan's skill. He immediately decided that this was the man his daughter must marry. Wajan explained that he was only a poor bird hunter and had no money to support his daughter. The King was impressed by his honesty. He promised Wajan money and invited him to come and live in the palace.

When Wajan and the princess met, they immediately fell in love with each other. A few weeks later, they were married. Raja Ishak held a big wedding feast for them.

He was so proud of Wajan that he asked him to
show off his skill as an archer. Poor Wajan
trembled. He knew he would be found out as a
cheat. He pretended he had left his bow and
arrow at home.
The King insisted
he use his.

Wajan was now shaking with terror. He didn't even know how to hold the bow and arrow properly! The guests became impatient. Some of them began to suspect that Wajan was a fraud.

Suddenly, one of them slapped Wajan on the back to hurry him up. This jolted Wajan's hand and he released the arrow. It sped through the air. Just at that moment a crane flew by. The arrow hit and killed it.

Raja Ishak quickly picked the dead bird up. He proudly announced to everyone that Wajan's arrow had pierced the crane's narrow neck. Everyone agreed that Wajan was the finest archer they had ever seen! But Wajan pretended to be angry.

"Your Majesty," he said, "I believe in shooting birds in the eye. That knock on my back made me kill the poor crane through the neck. I vow I will never shoot another bird again."

And from that time on Wajan was never asked to use a bow and arrow. He remained happily married to the King's daughter and continued to be known as the best archer in the land!

PRINCESS ALITAPTAP

L ong ago, in a beautiful valley at the foot of Mount Gayong in the Philippines, lived the people of the Pinak tribe. They led a happy and peaceful life. They grew rice and fruit on the fertile slopes of their valley. They hunted boar in the surrounding forests and caught fish in the nearby lake.

But this wonderful life did not last. One hot summer, no rain fell at all. The crops withered and the lake dried up. The Pinak people knew that unless rain fell, they would certainly starve to death.

So every night, all the people gathered to pray for rain to their god, Bathala. One night their prayers were answered. A golden chariot descended on the valley amid a blaze of gold and from it emerged a man and a woman.

"I am Bulan-hari and this is my wife Bitu-in," said the man. "Bathala has sent us to rule over you and to relieve you of your present suffering."

As he spoke, the heavens opened and rain lashed down upon the valley to water the crops and refill the lake with water. Good fortune once again returned to the Pinak tribe.

The years passed and everyone lived happily under the wise and caring rule of Bulan-hari and Bitu-in. A daughter was born to them during these years. She was a beautiful but unusual child, for she was born without a heart. A magic star in the centre of her forehead which sparkled like a precious jewel was all that kept her alive. The Pinak tribe gave her the name Alitaptap which means bright star.

Alitaptap grew up to be a very beautiful and graceful woman. Many young men fell in love with her, but Alitaptap rejected all of them because she had no heart and could feel no love for anyone.

Then one day, an old woman came to Bulan-hari's palace. She told him of a dream she had had, in which Pinak was destroyed by fire because the people no longer prayed to Bathala, their great god, to thank him for their good life.

Bulan-hari was terrified when he heard of her dream for he knew how dangerous it was to upset Bathala. "Tell me, wise woman, what can I do?" he asked.

"Alitaptap must marry," she replied.

Bulan-hari immediately called for his daughter
and told her what the old woman had said. "You
must get married, dear daughter," he said, "to save
the Pinak people and their beautiful valley."

Alitaptap heard his words but made no answer.
How could she? She had no heart and felt nothing,
no love and no sadness. Her father begged her over
and over again to agree to his wish, but Alitaptap
remained as still and as cold as a statue, completely
untouched by his words.

Bulan-hari lost his temper. Jumping up with his sword clutched in his hand, he swung it at Alitaptap! To his dismay and horror, it struck her on the forehead and shattered her magic star into a thousand tiny pieces.

Alitaptap fell to the floor. All life went out of her. Bulan-hari and Bitu-in wept bitterly for their daughter but their tears could not bring her back to life.

A few days later, just as the old woman had warned, Mount Gayong blew up. Red hot lava belched from its mouth and poured down the mountainside, drowning the valley below and all who lived in it.

When darkness fell, the mountain ceased its terrible revenge on Pinak. All that moved in the still night air were tiny sparks of light flitting to and fro. These glittering diamonds of light were really fireflies, but the people at the time believed they were the tiny fragments of Alitaptap's magic star.

To this day the people of the Philippines still call these sparkling fireflies Alitaptap, after the beautiful but heartless princess whose magic star remains scattered forever in the dark, dark nights and reminds them of life long ago in the Pinak Valley.

THE ANGRY GODS

Many years ago in Tibet, there lived a lovely young girl. Her name was Drolma. Every day, many men would pass by her house just to catch a glimpse of the beautiful Drolma.

Her parents worried about her. So many men wanted to marry their lovely daughter but they wanted to make sure that she married a good man.

Finally they decided to visit a temple to ask the gods for help. Unknown to them, a sly silk merchant called Kuban was listening to their conversation. And as he listened, an evil plan formed in his mind.

Early the next day, Kuban went to hide in the temple. The two old people came and prayed to the gods for advice. To their great surprise, a voice answered them immediately saying: "A man with a white cockerel will come to your house tomorrow. He is the man your daughter should marry."

Drolma's parents were so happy because they thought the gods had answered them. Little did they know it was really Kuban talking!

The next day, Kuban appeared at their house.
They were bitterly disappointed when they saw
him. He was so short, fat and ugly, and he had an
evil glint in his eyes! Poor Drolma! But the gods
had spoken and she had to go with him.

Kuban smuggled Drolma out of the village in
a basket. He didn't want anyone to know he
was taking the most beautiful girl in their
village away. But Kuban's home was in
another village several miles away.

Before long, his shoulders ached under the heavy burden of the basket. So he flopped down under a tree for a nap. He left poor Drolma in the basket.

Homesick and unhappy, she began to sob. A young hunter called Danam heard her sobbing and came to find out what the noise was. Imagine his surprise when he discovered Drolma in the basket!

She told him her sad tale. He realised that her parents had been tricked. "I'm taking you with me," he said, "and I'll leave Kuban my hunting dog as a little gift!" He put the dog in the basket and rode off with Drolma.

After a while, Kuban woke up. He trudged on home with his basket. He felt very excited as he opened it. But his excitement turned to terror as Danam's fierce dog sprang out and attacked him!

No one heard his screams. The next morning,
Kuban's neighbours found him dead. They
thought angry gods had killed him because there
was no trace of the dog anywhere. "Kuban has
upset the gods," they said, "and they have decided
to punish him."

Drolma, meanwhile, lived happily at Danam's house. As time went by, she and Danam fell in love. They decided to get married and sent for Drolma's parents.

Oh, how happy they were to see their lovely daughter again! And how relieved they were that she hadn't married Kuban. Danam was so kind and generous—and handsome too! He would make a fine husband for Drolma.

The next day, Drolma and Danam were married
amid great celebrations. They both looked so
happy together. But the happiest couple that day
was Drolma's parents. Their beloved daughter had
finally found a good husband. All thanks to the
gods who had so cleverly answered their prayer!

SOHRAB & RUSTUM

Long ago in Iran, there lived a famous warrior named Rustum. One day, his country was attacked by the Russians and he was asked to lead the troops into battle against them. Rustum immediately agreed but it saddened him to leave his beautiful wife, Tasmina, behind.

Before he left, he gave her a turquoise necklace. "Send this to me if you are in danger," he said, "and I will return immediately." Tasmina bade her husband a sad farewell.

Eight months later, she gave birth to a baby son whom she called Sohrab. She feared that her husband would want Sohrab to become a soldier one day like him. Then she would be left without a husband and a son. She therefore sent word to Rustum that they had a daughter.

Rustum was very disappointed to hear this as he had wanted a son. So he decided not to return home to Tasmina. He remained with his troops on the battlefield.

The years passed and Sohrab grew up to be a strong and brave young man. He heard lots of stories about his father's heroic deeds and longed to see him. He pleaded with his mother to let him find his father.

His mother finally agreed. Before he left, she gave him the turquoise necklace Rustum had given her. "Show this to your father," she said, "so he will know that you are his son."

Sohrab spent many months searching for Rustum. Then he thought of a way to get his father to come to him! He told some soldiers that he was the best soldier in Iran and that he wanted to prove it to Rustum. He knew that his proud father would not be able to resist such a challenge.

He was right! When Rustum heard about this arrogant young soldier, he agreed to meet Sohrab in single combat. A few days later, the two met on the battlefield.

Sohrab tried to tell his father that he was his son but Rustum refused to listen. "I have no son," he cried. "Talk no more young man. You need all your strength to do battle with me!"

And with these words he charged at Sohrab with his spear. The clash of steel rang out as Sohrab defended himself. Time and again Rustum nearly sliced his son in two with his razor sharp sword, but Sohrab moved quickly out of the way.

As the fight wore on, Rustum became more and more weary. For a moment he seemed to falter and Sohrab, feeling anxious for his father, lowered his shield. In a flash, Rustum lunged at him and cut him down with one sweep of his sword! He waved proudly to his soldiers while his son lay dying at his feet.

Then Sohrab took out the necklace his mother had given him and weakly whispered, "Do you remember this, my father? Now will you believe that I am your son?"

Rustum recognised the necklace at once and knew that Sohrab was telling the truth. He flung himself down beside his dying son and wept bitterly. "Do not weep for me," Sohrab sighed. "Weep for my mother who has lost a son. Promise me you will return home and live with her for the rest of your life."

Rustum bowed his head in sorrow. He gave Sohrab his word he would always take care of Tasmina. On hearing this, Sohrab died with a peaceful smile on his lips.

From that day on, Rustum never touched a sword again. He returned to his beloved Tasmina and begged her forgiveness. And for the rest of his life, he mourned the death of his brave young son.

THE RED HILL

Many years ago, wild swordfish filled the sea around Singapore. The people were very afraid of these fierce fish. They attacked fishermen out at sea and scared people away from the beaches.

At this time, Raja Iskander was the ruler of
Singapore. He decided that something must be
done. He ordered his soldiers to kill the swordfish.

The soldiers waited on the beach for the tide to come in. Then they tried to stab the fish with their sharp spears. But the swordfish defeated them. They killed and injured many brave soldiers and the sea ran red with their blood.

The Raja was horrified that so many soldiers had died. He walked sadly back up the beach. "What can I do to stop these dreadful swordfish?" he exclaimed aloud.

"I have an idea," said a little voice. The Raja turned around and saw a young boy sitting on a rock. "Build a wall of banana stems in the water," said the little boy. "Then when the fish come in on the tide, their sharp swords will pierce the soft stems and they will be trapped."

What a great idea, the Raja thought. So he ordered his soldiers to cut down all the banana trees they could find. Then they built a long wall of banana stems along the beach.

At high tide, the fish swam towards the shore and their swords stuck fast to the sticky stems of the banana trees. The soldiers quickly killed the trapped fish. What a feast of fish the people had that day! No soldiers had died and no swordfish remained to frighten them. The people felt safe and happy again.

The Raja, however, felt uneasy. "That little boy is too clever," he told his Captain. "I fear he will be more powerful than me one day."

The Captain thought the Raja wanted him to get rid of the boy. The next night, he ordered four men to kill the little boy. They crept up the hill to the boy's hut and kicked the door open.

To their surprise, they found a strange old woman with long white hair there. The boy was nowhere to be seen. "You wicked men," she screamed. "The boy helped you and yet you want to kill him. I will punish you all!"

The terrified soldiers fled at once. Suddenly a hole opened up in the ground before them! Thick red blood gushed from it and streamed down the hill after them. It stained the ground red. From that day on, the hill has been called Red Hill or Bukit Merah.

Strangely enough, the old woman and the little boy were never seen again. It is said that until the little boy returns, the hill will remain the colour of blood to remind people of the evil plot to kill an innocent boy who saved so many lives.

THE CHESS PLAYER

On the grassy pasturelands of Mongolia, there once lived two boys called Tohan and Benppo. Benppo's father was a wealthy sheep farmer. He wanted his son to remain at home and work on the farm with him. Tohan's father was a poor weaver. He wanted a better life for his son and so he decided to send him into the town to study.

Tohan was very excited. He ran to tell his friend Benppo the news. "My father is sending me away to study," he said. "He wants me to learn how to read and write, play the flute and learn the game of chess. Wouldn't it be nice if you could come too?"

"What's the good of studying?" Benppo asked. "My father doesn't know how to do all those things and see how successful he is. One day I will be a wealthy sheep farmer too. I don't need to study like you."

So, saying goodbye to his father and friends, Tohan went into the town alone. There he learnt how to read and write, play the flute and the game of chess. As he was a clever and hard-working boy, it didn't take him long to master all three. Then he decided to go home.

When he returned, he found his father had died. Worse still, bandits suddenly arrived and captured his camp. They took everyone prisoner, including Tohan and Benppo! Tohan pleaded with the bandits to release them.

"Why?" asked the bandits. "Do you have a special skill that makes you better than a bandit?"

"I can play the flute," offered Tohan. He took out his flute and put it to his mouth. Sweet, soothing melodies filled the camp and slowly the bandits hard faces softened into smiles.

The leader of the bandits walked over to Tohan when he stopped playing and said, "For playing such fine music you can go free tomorrow morning."

"Please, could you free my friend Benppo too?" begged Tohan.

"Only if he can do something as well as you can play the flute," answered the bandit leader. But Benppo sadly admitted he could do nothing very well. "So stay with us then," said the leader. "For those who are no good at anything make excellent bandits!"

Tohan travelled on alone to a small town. It was owned by a wealthy landlord who employed everyone living there. He was the only person in town who could read and write. Every week, he signed for just small handfuls of food at the local store to pay everyone.

Tohan decided to help these people. He wrote the landlord's name on large orders of food for them. That week they had more food than they had ever had before! They were very grateful to Tohan but made him leave in case the landlord killed him for helping them.

So Tohan rode on until he came to the tiny kingdom of Sakhim. He was surprised to see so many people playing chess. He discovered that the King of Sakhim was crazy about the game. Every day, he would play against one of his subjects. But if they lost to him, they were put to death!

Tohan felt very angry about this and rode on to find the King. To his surprise he found Benppo being held prisoner outside the King's tent. He had escaped from the bandits only to be caught by the King of Sakhim's soldiers. Furthermore, he was to be the King's next opponent and he had no idea how to play chess!

Tohan joined the large crowd which had gathered to watch the match. In just two minutes the King had won! He jumped to his feet ready to slice Benppo in two with his massive sword.

Your Majesty, wait!" cried Tohan. "Before killing this man, I beg you to have a game of chess with me. If I lose, you can kill both of us."

The King was delighted at the thought of playing another game that day. He also liked the idea of killing two men at the same time! So he invited Tohan to sit down to play.

"But if I win," continued Tohan, "then you must grant me any wish."

The King laughed, "What a foolish young man you are to think you can beat me. But yes, if you win, I will grant you anything you wish."

The crowd fell silent and the two men began to play. The King was good but Tohan was even better and eventually won the game. The King flew into a terrible rage but had to keep his promise because so many people had heard him making it. To the cheers of the crowd, Tohan asked the King to do away with the death sentence in Sakhim. The King reluctantly agreed and then set Benppo free.

Sakhim was a very happy place from that time on and so, too, was Tohan. At last he had put all his learning to good use—just as his father had hoped he would do!

THE DRAGON OF KINABALU

Long ago, on the top of Mount Kinabalu in Borneo, there lived a dragon. He owned a large and beautiful pearl. Every day, he played with it, rolling it back and forth like a ball. People believed he controlled the weather with it.

The Emperor of China came to hear of this pearl and decided he wanted it. He sent his two sons, Wee Ping and Wee San, to Borneo to steal it. The princes, together with one hundred soldiers, set sail for Borneo in twelve sailing junks.

When they arrived in Borneo, they set out immediately to find the famous mountain. Their journey up the rugged slopes of Mount Kinabalu proved very difficult. The dragon guarded his cave very fiercely and killed many of their soldiers.

Then Wee San had a clever idea. He climbed a tall tree so he could see the dragon's cave. He noted what time the dragon left his cave to hunt for food and what time he returned to it.

Next he ordered his men to make a fake pearl and a large kite. He waited until the dragon left his cave. Then he placed the fake pearl in a bag, slung it across his shoulder and flew up to the mountain-top on the kite. He exchanged the real pearl for the fake one, and then his brother pulled his kite back to the ground.

The brothers quickly returned to their ships and set sail for China. Meanwhile, the dragon returned to his cave. He began to play with the pearl. He soon realised it was a fake! With a snort of fire he slithered down the mountainside and crashed into the sea. He swam furiously after the brothers' ships.

Fortunately Wee San saw him coming. He quickly thought of another clever plan. He ordered his soldiers to heat up a cannon ball until it glowed red hot. Then he fired it at the dragon. The angry beast thought it was his pearl and swallowed it in one gulp! He gave a blood-curdling roar. And then, squirming in pain, he sank slowly beneath the waves.

The brothers continued their journey and sailed
safely home. The Emperor was thrilled with
the pearl and gave a big party to celebrate his
sons' return. Wee Ping told everyone about their
adventure but he never once mentioned Wee San's
clever ideas. Wee San was hurt but he kept quiet.
He loved his elder brother and didn't want to
embarrass him in front of so many people.

The Emperor was so pleased he gave Wee Ping the dragon's pearl to keep. However he had noticed how quiet his younger son had been. He realised Wee San must have helped his older brother steal the pearl. So he had a magnificent copy made and gave it to Wee San saying, "Do not be unhappy that your brother has the genuine pearl. Remember, the love between brothers is worth more than all the pearls in thc world."

Wee San was grateful for his father's kind gift and for his wise words. He never told anyone how unfair Wee Ping had been but he still felt sad at the way his brother had treated him. So one day he decided to leave China and seek a new life elsewhere.

He set sail for Borneo and arrived in the land of Brunei. He was warmly welcomed by the Sultan of Brunei who immediately liked the gentle Chinese prince. Over the years, they became the best of friends.

Wee San also fell in love with the Sultan's lovely daughter. On the day they were married, the Sultan named Wee San the successor to his throne. Wee San realised what happiness he had found in Brunei even though he had lost the dragon's pearl to his brother.

Wee Ping, on the other hand, never found real happiness. His life was very empty without Wee San and the dragon's pearl never made up for the loss of his brother's love and friendship.

LORD KRISHNA'S FLUTE

A long, long time ago, the god Vishnu came to Earth and became Lord Krishna. As a young man, Krishna loved to play the flute. He often went for walks in the forests and played for the animals there. They loved his beautiful music.

One day, after he had played for them, he fell asleep. He didn't know it but a young boy in ragged clothes had also been listening to his music. When he saw that Krishna was asleep, he crept up to Krishna's side and took the flute. He put it to his lips and tried to play it, but try as he might, he could not play a single tune. All he could produce were odd, sharp notes which soon woke Krishna up.

L ord Krishna was very angry. "How dare you steal my flute!" he cried. "I am the Lord Krishna. Surely you know that no one can touch anything belonging to the gods. You must be punished!"

The poor boy fell to his knees. "Oh, my Lord Krishna," he wept, "I had no idea that you were a god. I did not steal your flute. I only wanted to try and play it as beautifully as you."

Lord Krishna felt sorry for the boy, so he decided to soften the punishment. "Come, my boy," he said, and gently put his hands over the boy's mouth. "From this time on, you will try to copy my song but you will never succeed." Then he touched the boy's rags and whispered, "You will also wear my colours and stay in these forests forever."

And with these words, the boy turned into a beautiful bird with the blue markings of Krishna and began to sing the song of Krishna's flute. But as Lord Krishna had foretold, it couldn't finish the song. The bird became known as the Whistling Thrush of Malabar. To this day, it is still trying to finish the lovely song played by Krishna on his magic flute.